PICTURE MAZE

PUZZLES FOR A
ROAD TRIP

Conceptis
Puzzles

JUNIOR

PUZZLE WRIGHT JUNIOR New York

An Imprint of Sterling Publishing Co., Inc.
1166 Avenue of the Americas
New York, NY 10036

Puzzles in this book previously appeared in *Picture This! Mazes*,
Hidden Picture Mazes, *Secret Picture Mazes*, and *Sneaky Picture Mazes*

ISBN 978-1-4549-3160-7

Distributed in Canada by Sterling Publishing Co., Inc.
c/o Canadian Manda Group, 664 Annette Street
Toronto, Ontario M6S 2C8, Canada
Distributed in the United Kingdom by GMC Distribution Services
Castle Place, 166 High Street, Lewes, East Sussex BN7 1XU, England
Distributed in Australia by NewSouth Books,
University of New South Wales, Sydney, NSW 2052, Australia

For information about custom editions, special sales, and premium and
corporate purchases, please contact Sterling Special Sales at 800-805-5489
or specialsales@sterlingpublishing.com.

Manufactured in Canada
Lot #:
2 4 6 8 10 9 7 5 3 1
04/19

sterlingpublishing.com
puzzlewright.com

Cover design by Valerie Hou

Introduction

Solve a maze and create a picture!

There are two types of picture maze puzzles in this book, basic and reversed. To start out, solve each of these fun puzzles just as you would a traditional maze: find the true path by starting at the maze's entrance and drawing a line to the maze's exit, avoiding incorrect paths and dead ends.

But the fun is not over once you exit! What's next? In the basic kind of maze, you color in the path you traced with a dark, thick line of pen or marker to create a picture. In the other kind, which we call the reversed maze, after you have traced the true path lightly in pencil, color in all the *incorrect* paths with a thick pen or marker to create your picture. (You can tell the difference between the two kinds of maze by the color of the triangles at the entrance and exit. Basic mazes have black triangles and reversed mazes have white triangles. Just remember, the color of the path matches the color of the arrows.)

You might be surprised to learn that picture mazes of this kind were invented in Japan over 35 years ago. Today picture mazes have a dedicated following among children and adults all over the world. So grab your marker and pencil and get started!

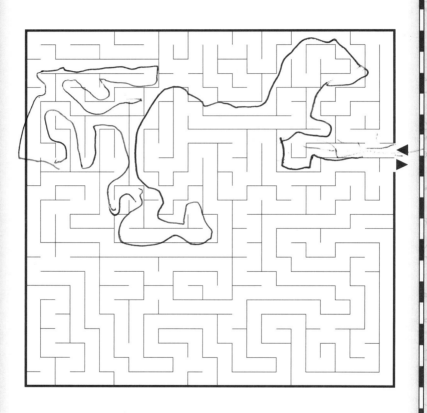

Answer, Page 78

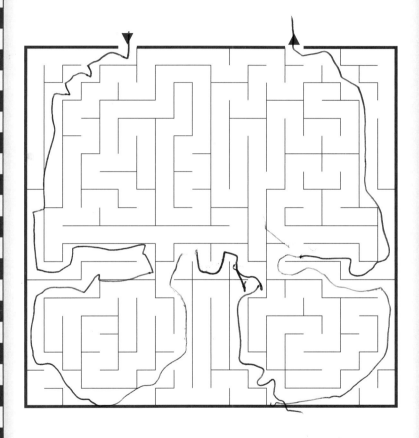

Answer, Page 78

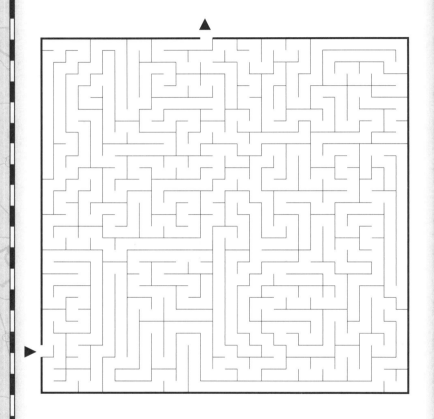

Answer, Page 78

4

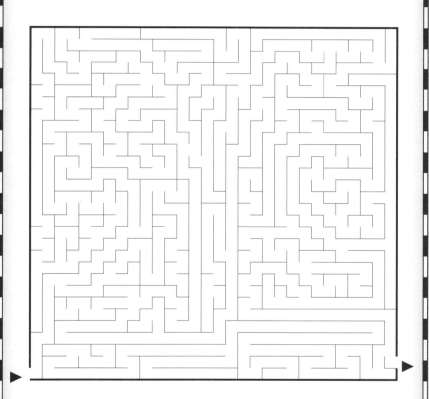

Answer, Page 78

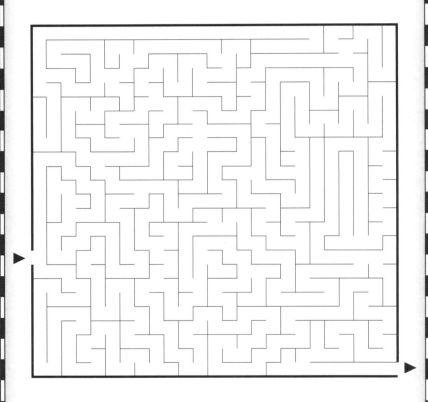

Answer, Page 79

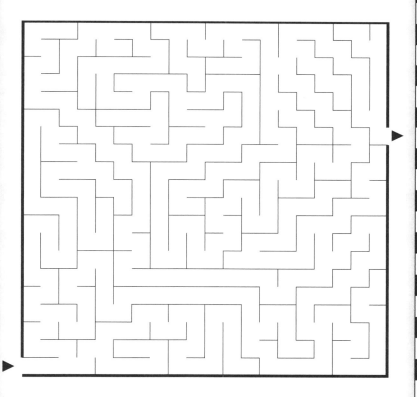

Answer, Page 79

Answer, Page 79

Answer, Page 79

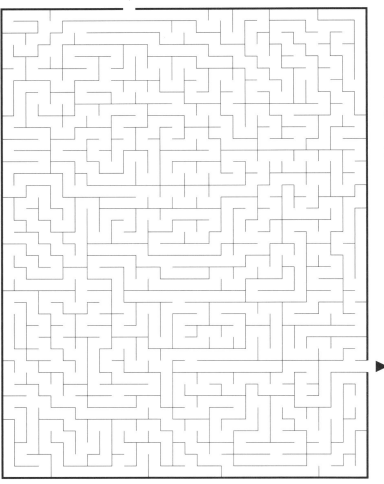

Answer, Page 80

Answer, Page 80

Answer, Page 80

Answer, Page 80

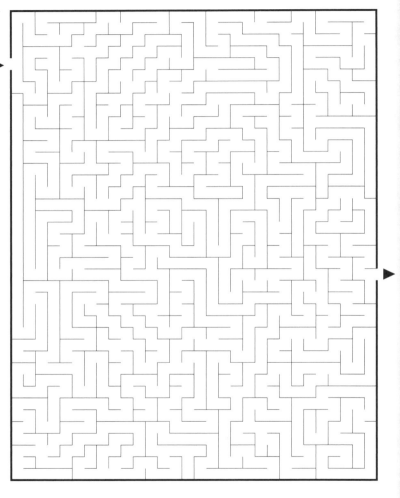

Answer, Page 81

Answer, Page 81

Answer, Page 81

Answer, Page 81

Answer, Page 82

Answer, Page 82

Answer, Page 82

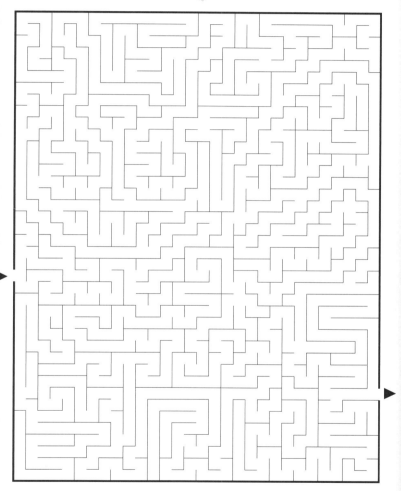

Answer, Page 82

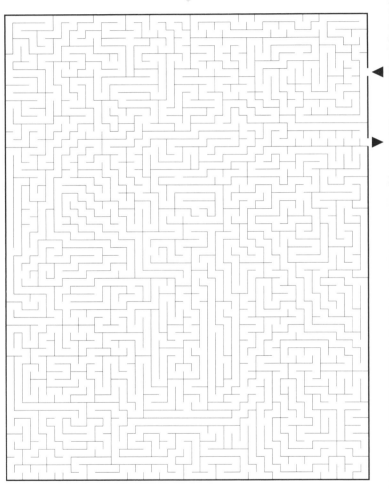

Answer, Page 83

Answer, Page 83

23

Answer, Page 84

Answer, Page 84

25

Answer, Page 84

Answer, Page 84

Answer, Page 84

28

Answer, Page 84

Answer, Page 85

Answer, Page 85

Answer, Page 85

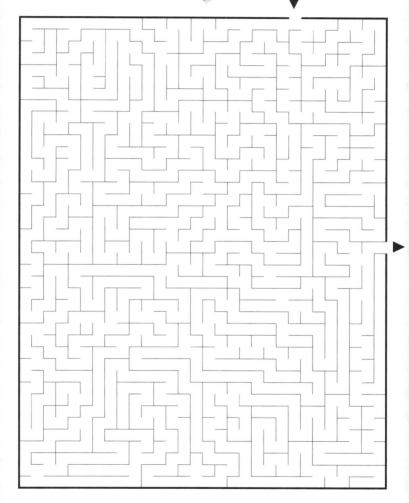

Answer, Page 85

33

Answer, Page 86

Answer, Page 86

35

Answer, Page 86

Answer, Page 86

37

Answer, Page 87

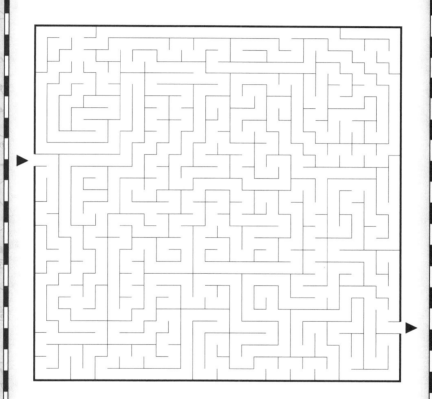

Answer, Page 87

Answer, Page 87

Answer, Page 87

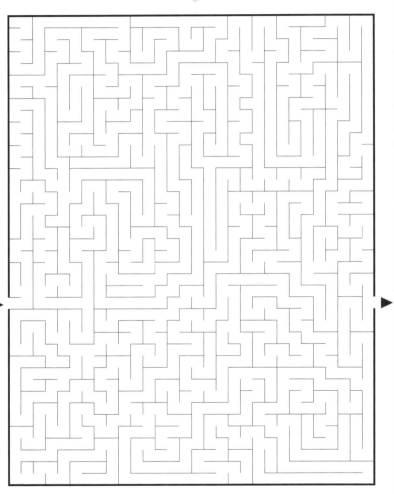

Answer, Page 88

42

Answer, Page 88

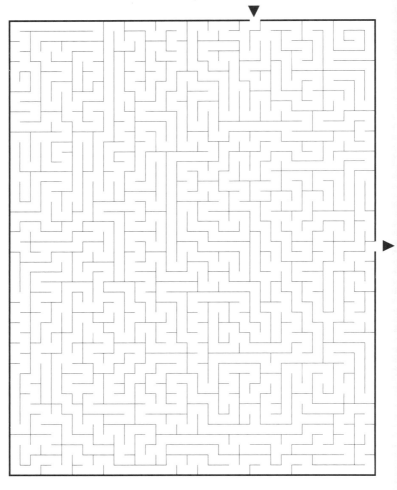

Answer, Page 88

▽ △

Answer, Page 88

Answer, Page 89

46

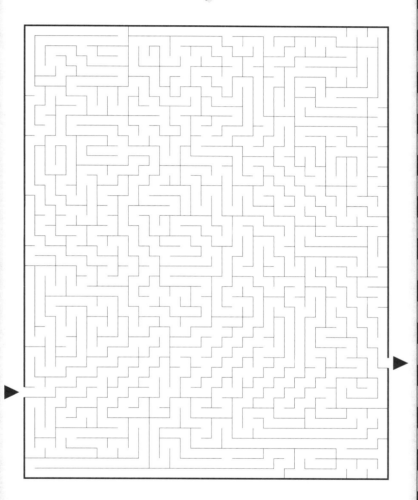

Answer, Page 89

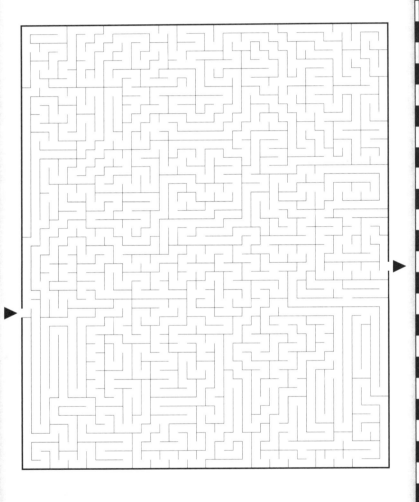

Answer, Page 89

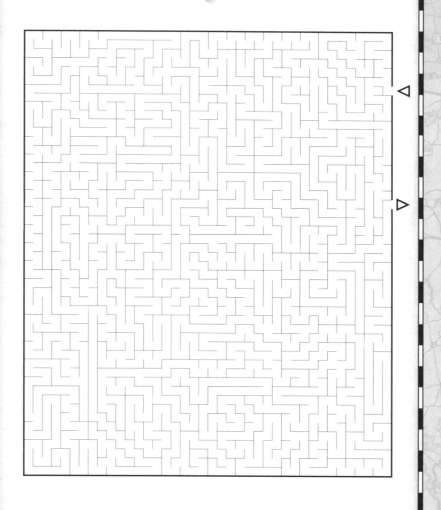

Answer, Page 89

Answer, Page 90

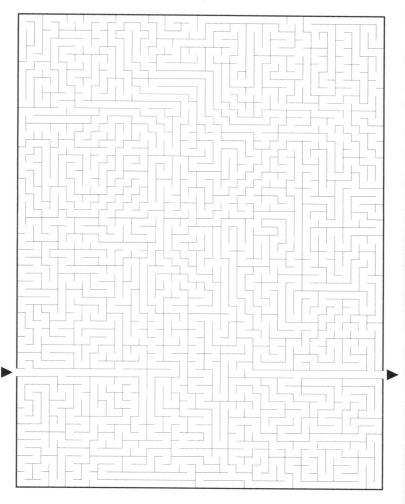

Answer, Page 90

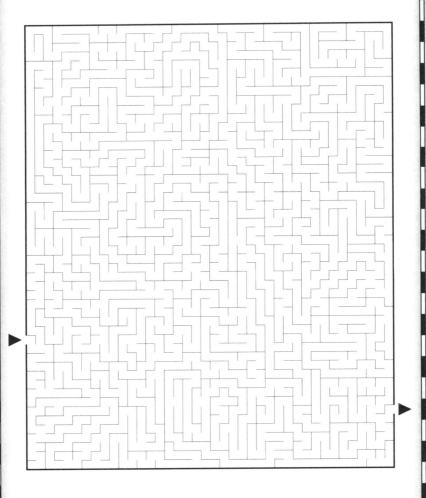

Answer, Page 90

52

Answer, Page 90

53

Answer, Page 91

Answer, Page 91

55

Answer, Page 91

Answer, Page 91

57

Answer, Page 92

Answer, Page 92

Answer, Page 92

60

Answer, Page 92

61

Answer, Page 93

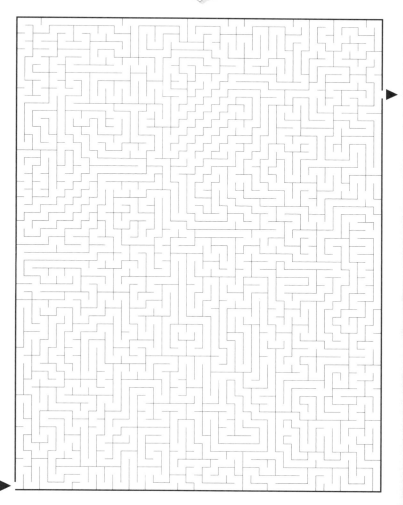

62

Answer, Page 93

63

Answer, Page 93

Answer, Page 94

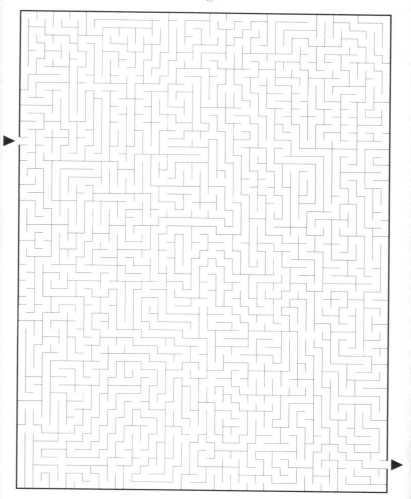

Answer, Page 94

Answer, Page 94

Answer, Page 94

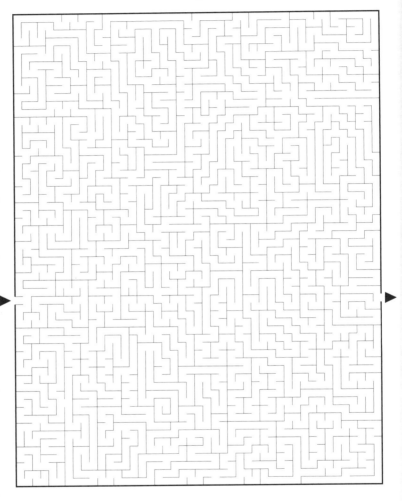

Answer, Page 95

Answer, Page 95

71

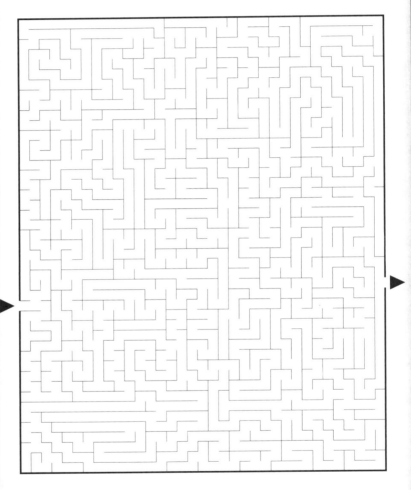

Answer, Page 95

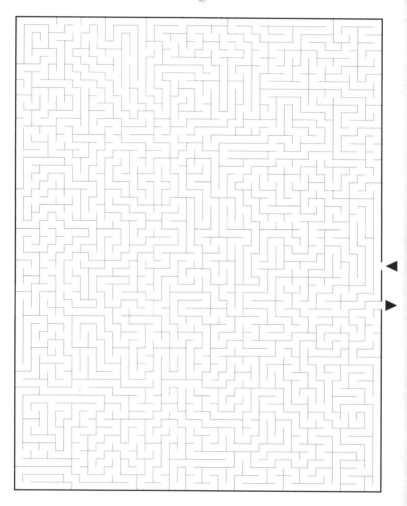

Answer, Page 96

Answer, Page 96

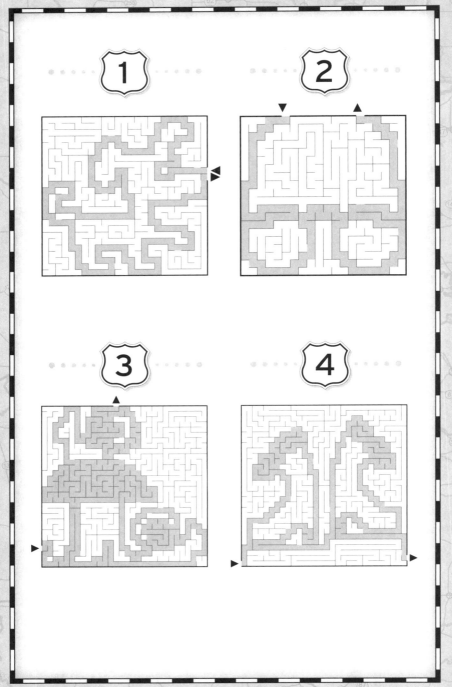

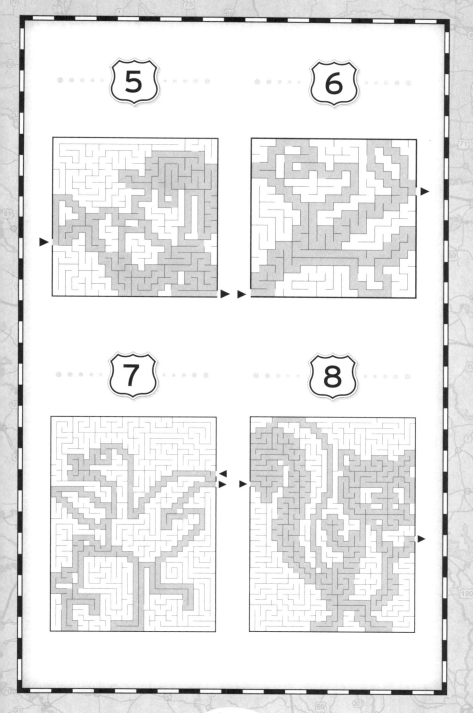

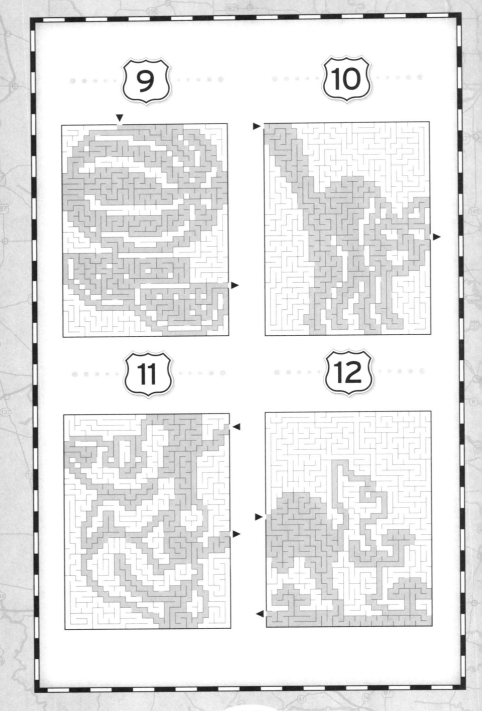

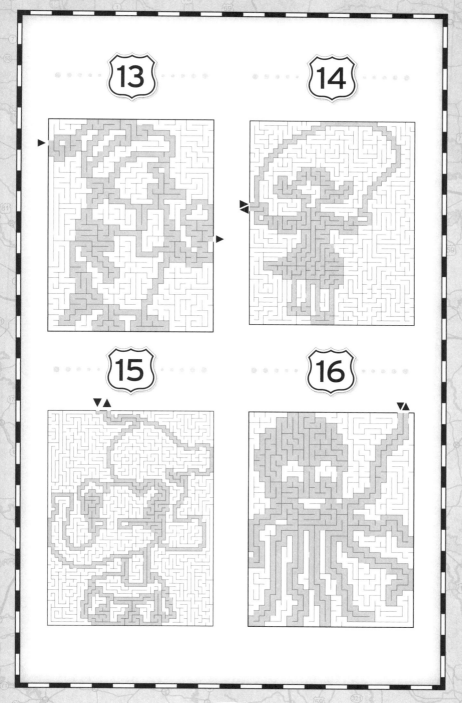

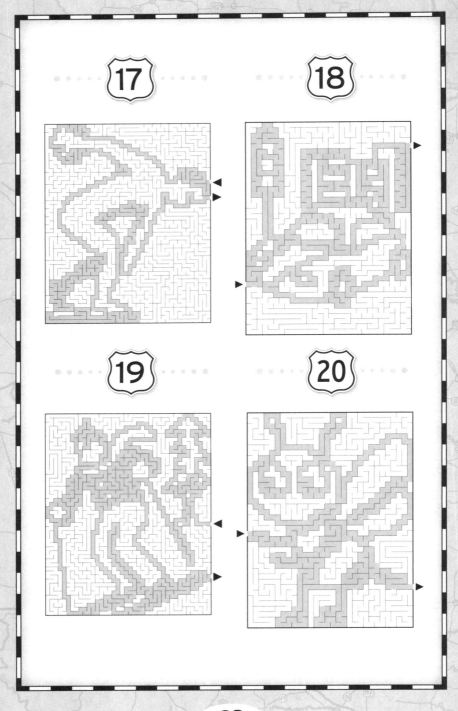

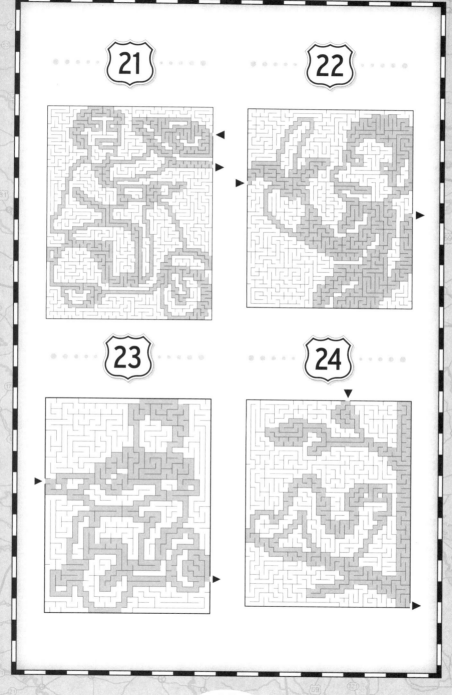

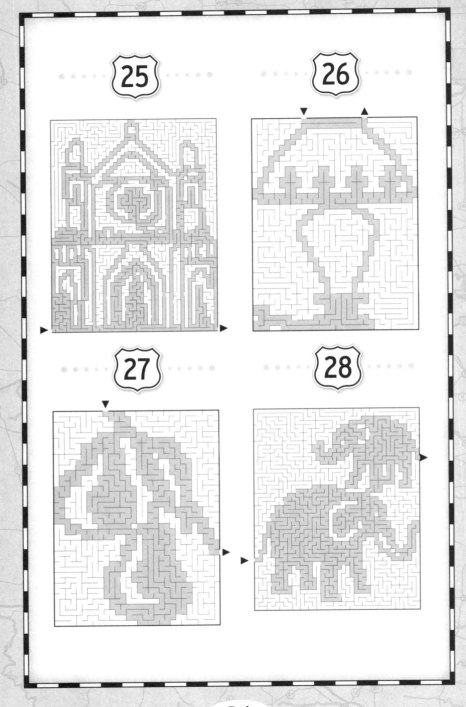

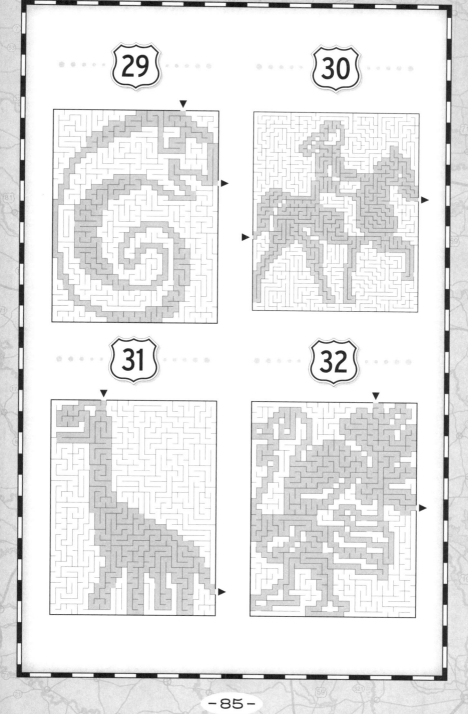

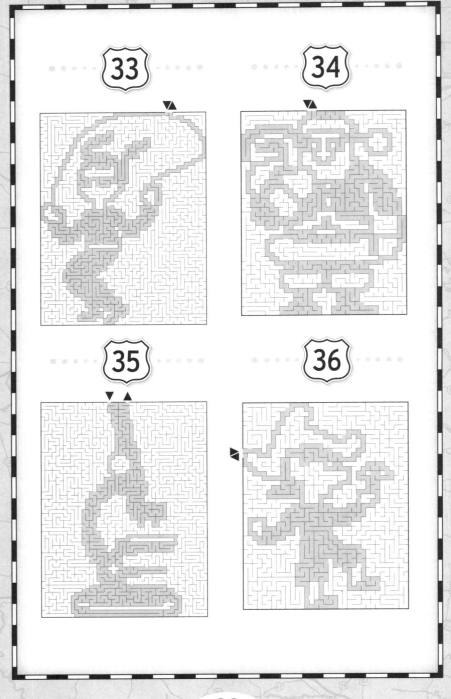

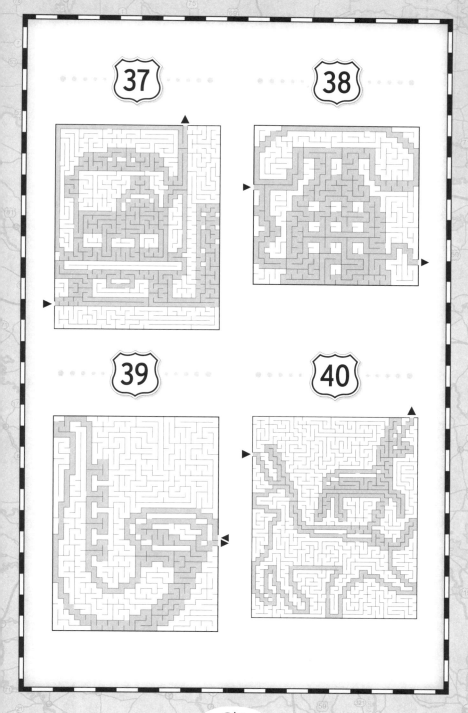

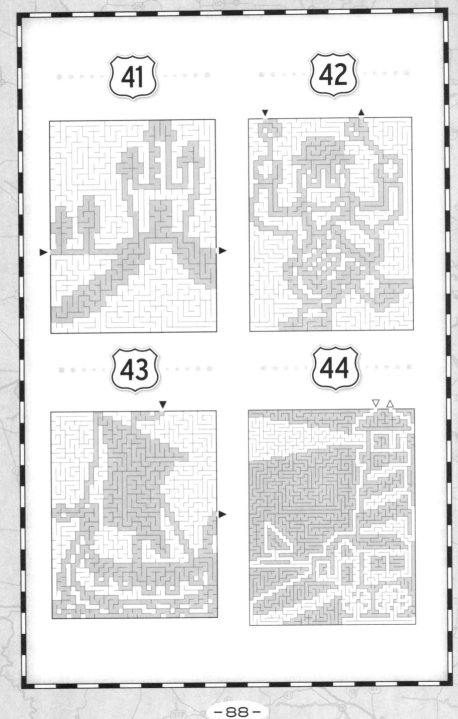

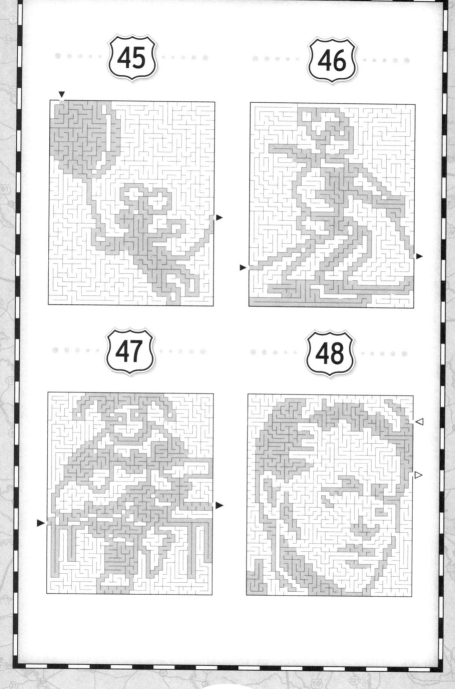

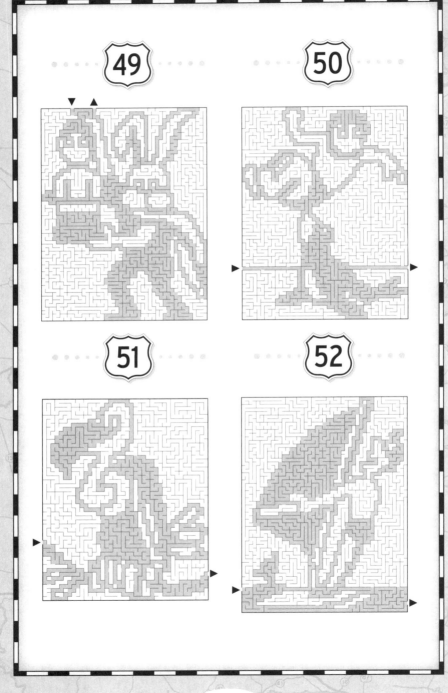

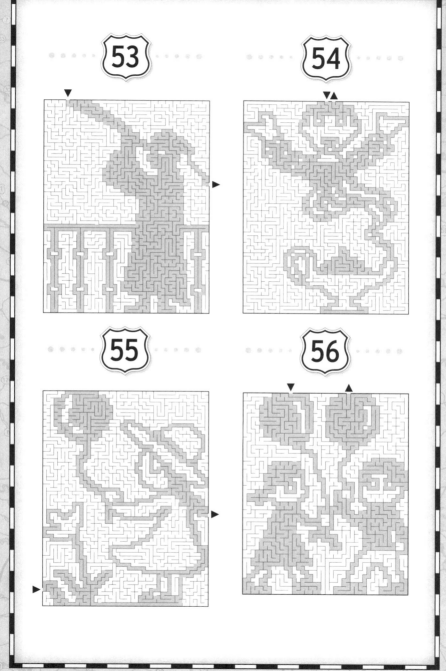

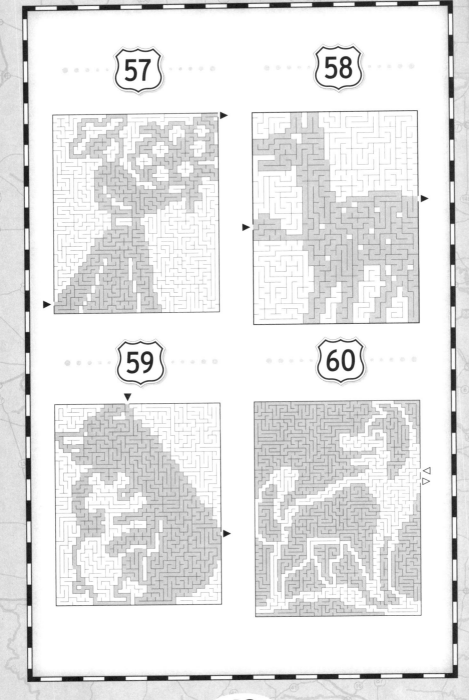

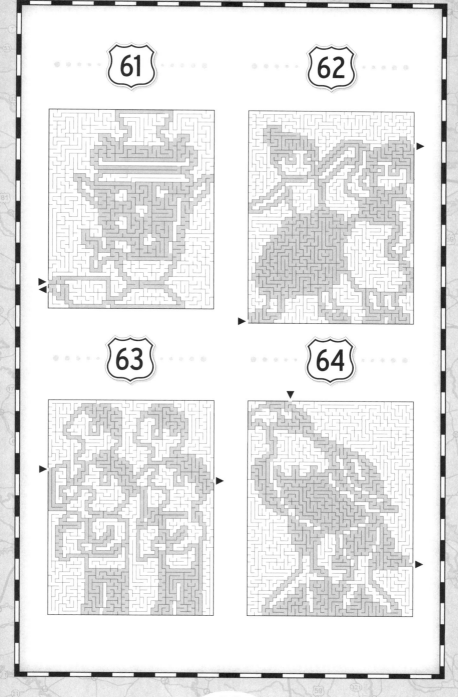

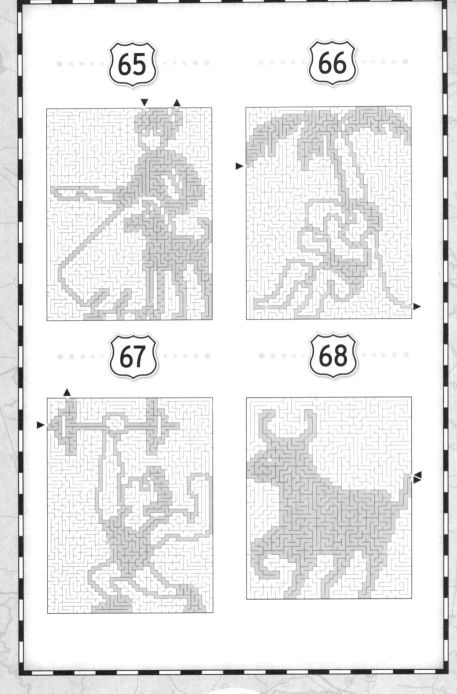

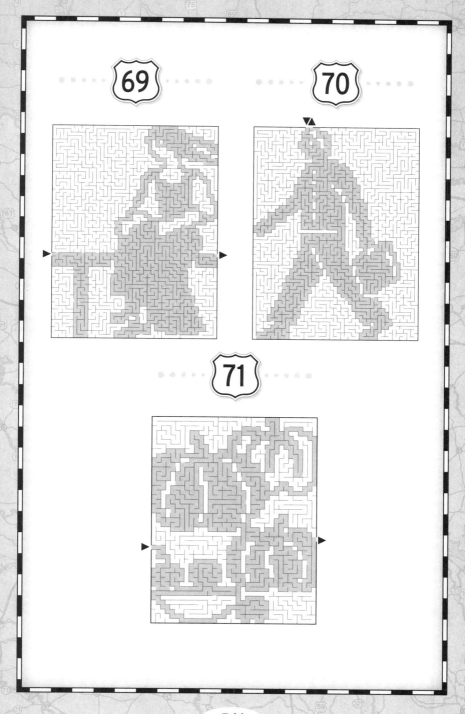

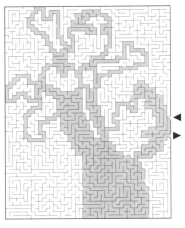